This Journal Belongs To:

Name _

Address _

_ _

Phone _

Email _

We hope you enjoyed using this book. It would really help us a lot if you would take a moment to leave a review. Thanks!

Snippy Chuckles Journals
Ha! Ha! Very Funny!
Ready for another chuckle?
Check out our book catalog at:

amazon.com/author/snippychucklesjournals